THIS BOOK BELONGS TO
The Library of

....

....

@COPYRIGHT 2024

The content contained within this book may not be reproduced, duplicated, or transmitted without direct written permission from the author or the publisher. Under no circumstances will any blame or legal responsibility be held against the publisher, or author, for any damages, reparation, or monetary loss due to the information contained within this book. Either directly or indirectly.

Legal Notice:

This book is copyright protected. This book is only for personal use. You cannot amend, distribute, sell, use, quote, or paraphrase any part, or the content within this book, without the consent of the author or publisher.

Disclaimer Notice:

Please note the information contained within this document is for educational and entertainment purposes only. All effort has been executed to present accurate, up-to-date, and reliable, complete information. No warranties of any kind are declared or implied. Readers acknowledge that the author is not engaging in the rendering of legal, financial, medical, or professional advice. The content within this book has been derived from various sources. Please consult a licensed professional before attempting any techniques outlined in this book. By reading this document, the reader agrees that under no circumstances is the author responsible for any losses, direct or indirect, which are incurred as a result of the use of the information contained within this document, including, but not limited to — errors, omissions, or inaccuracies.

Did you like my book? I pondered it severely before releasing this book. Although the response has been overwhelming, it is always pleasing to see, read or hear a new comment. Thank you for reading this and I would love to hear your honest opinion about it. Furthermore, many people are searching for a unique book, and your feedback will help me gather the right books for my reading audience.

Thanks!

Table of Contents

INTRODUCTION	5
Should You Make A Career Change?	7
Common Mistakes People Make When Changing Careers	12
SWOT Analysis	17
Picking the Right Career Path	25
Opportunities Available To You	29
Hot Jobs	36
What Comes Next	52
Saying Goodbye To Your Job	59
Finding and Getting That New Job	63
Turning a Hobby into a Career	75
Conclusion	78

INTRODUCTION

Whether you are newly graduated from high school or currently employed in a job you hate and want something else, choosing a career is a very important decision. This writer knows especially well about this and it's a decision that shouldn't be made lightly and simply isn't easy to do in the first place.

When you're young, you have a myriad of choices ahead of you, but really do at any age. It doesn't matter how young or old you are, you can still make a career choice that can make you happy and enhance your life even if it's a drastic one!

With all the different occupations to choose from, where do you even begin to find something that you will be good at doing and love doing as well? The truth is, all you have to do is look at yourself and inside yourself to see where you should be. Plenty of people have made career changes late in life.

Grandma Moses began her painting career well into her 80's and because one of the most well-respected painters in the art world. Many professional athletes HAVE to make career choices once they are no longer able to play sports at a level they always have been able to. Stay-at-home moms with children in school suddenly find themselves wanting to do something worthwhile instead of staying home all day. Some of them have even built hobbies into multi-millionaire businesses!

It happens all the time and for a variety of different reasons. The world's business economy is volatile at the very least and many companies have to lay off workers or close the business entirely. That leaves displaced worked facing career moves they hadn't anticipated. In fact, the reality is that the average person will make 2 to 5 career changes between the time they enter the work force to the time when they retire.

Many colleges have displaced workers programs and adult education programs that can ease people into a career change. Sometimes, however, the best way to make a career change is just to jump in and do it. But how do you know what career to choose? That's why you're reading this book. We can help guide you toward the perfect career for you. We'll provide guidelines for you to consider and questions that you need to ask.

The career of your dreams could be right around the corner and it's time you went after it!

Chapter 1

Should You Make A Career Change?

(Return to Contents)

Many people don't like their jobs – it is part of being in the working world. Even people who claim to love their jobs still have days when the thought of going to work can be just too much to bear. However, the truth is that you just may be on the wrong career path if your level of job satisfaction is less than what it should be.

The best way to really see and accept that it might be time for a career change is to honestly look at how you feel about what you do. This is really a very easy process. All you need to do is keep a daily work journal.

First, record how you feel about going into the office or workplace every day. Be honest with yourself and write your true feelings. Are you dreading walking through the doors and the thought of it makes you nauseous? Maybe you're looking forward to it but once you get there, you find that you are bored and unable to concentrate.

When a specific job situation comes up, write down your reactions to having to complete that task. Your boss has given you the assignment of researching past profit margins for one of the products your company produces. He wants a comprehensive report done and on his desk within two days. Are you angry and dreading the job or does it make you happy to be trusted with an important job? Write it down!

In your work journal, jot down your feelings about your co-workers. Do you generally get along with everyone, or do you find yourself constantly at odds with people or a specific person?

The key to a work journal is to write down exactly how you feel about various aspects of your job and then look for recurring themes. Are you unhappy because of the people you are around or because of what you are doing? Perhaps you just disagree with specific company policies. After you have identified the reason that you are unhappy with your job, you can start to take steps to look for something else.

Still not sure if you should make a career change? OK, then it's time for a little quiz. Ask yourself the following questions and answer true or false:

1. There are few opportunities for growth within your company.

2. You find the work you are doing boring.

3. Few jobs exist in your field.

4. You want to earn more money than you ever will in your current field.

5. You will need to upgrade your skills to stay in your current field, but you aren't satisfied enough to even make the effort.

6. You want to do something more with your life.

7. You want to pursue a lifelong passion.

8. There's a new career you want to pursue. After doing your research, it seems to be a good fit for you.

9. You want to work in a field that will utilize your talents, skills, and education and your current occupation doesn't do this.

10. Your life has changed since you first got into this career and now the requirements of your job don't mix well with your current

situation (extensive travel when you now have children at home)

11. Your occupation is too stressful.

Look at your answers to the above questions. Are you finding that you have more "True" answers? If so, then a career change is probably in order. But let's look at why according to your answer to each question.

1. If you want the opportunity to grow your career, it's important to be in a company that will allow you to do that. Perhaps you want greater responsibilities or a position higher up on the corporate ladder — things you won't have if you stick with your current occupation.

2. People can get bored with their work. Before you change careers, you may want to make sure it's your occupation in general that is boring you and not just your current job. If it is your occupation, you should consider a career change.

3. When there are few jobs available in your field, a career change truly might be in order. Since opportunities are limited you may want to start exploring other occupations that have a better outlook.

4. A lot of people want to earn more money. Keep in mind happiness does not come with higher earnings. However, if your career is unfulfilling for other reasons, you might want to change careers.

5. Upgrading your skills in order to stay in your current occupation will take some effort. If you aren't satisfied with your career anyway, you may want to start exploring other options rather than stress about what you need to do but don't have the desire or motivation to do.

6. In general, if you find your career unfulfilling, that's the number one reason to find a new career. Being happy with your job can contribute greatly to personal fulfillment which is something we all

need, so definitely make a career change if you say "True" to this question.

7. If you want to pursue your lifelong passion, by all means, go for it or at least consider it as an option. Make sure you do your homework first, though, to ascertain this career is the right choice.

8. As long as you've researched a possible new career choice, there's really no reason you shouldn't go for it if it seems like something that will make you happy. In fact, this is a no-brainer – of course you should change your career here!

9. There's a reason why you got an education in the first place. Because you wanted to do a specific type of work. Maybe you just have a specific flair to perform certain tasks but your current job doesn't use those talents. Why would you stick around?

10. If your life has changed significantly since you first began your career and it is causing your personal life to be at odds with your business life, you'll have to make a choice. Unless you want to do nothing but work, you really should choose personal happiness.

11. There's enough stress in life without your work contributing to it. Before you decide to change careers, you should figure out whether it's your occupation that's stressful or just your particular place of employment. If it is your occupation, change careers.

Of course, making a job change is never easy. Having a regular paycheck and job security is important – there's no doubt about that. But if you're unhappy in your job and feeling unfulfilled, are you doing yourself a favor by staying there? We spend a lot of our time working, so it really is important that you do something with that time that is meaningful for you and will enhance your life rather than inhibit it.

Before you make the leap to change your career path, you will want to avoid some common mistakes that many people make. By knowing what those mistakes are, you'll know what NOT to do when undertaking such a life-changing event such as exploring a new career.

Chapter 2

Common Mistakes People Make When Changing Careers

(Return to Contents)

Making a complete career change, whatever the reason, is a really big undertaking that can have huge ramifications in your life if you don't take the time to think things through. Jumping too quickly can result in more unhappiness in your career than you're feeling right now, so it's important to avoid making a few common mistakes.

First, have a plan. Probably the biggest mistake you can make is attempting to change careers without a plan. A successful career change can often take months to accomplish when you have a strategy, so without one, you could end up adrift for an even longer period.

Having a detailed action plan (including items such as strategies, finances, research, and education/training) is essential to your success. Without a plan, you might take the first job offer that comes along, whether it is a good fit for you or not.

Don't make the mistake of confusing hating your current job with hating your current career. Take the time to analyze whether it's just the job, another employee, or your boss that you hate, or whether it's the career, the skills necessary to do the job, or the work that you dislike.

The same goes with if you are feeling bored or lost with your job; review whether it's the job, the employer, or the career. Whatever you determine, it's best not to leave your job -- if possible -- until you have a plan for finding a new career.

Many people make career changes based solely on the prospect of making more money or because of better benefits. This, too, can be a mistake. Certain career fields are very alluring because of the salary and other benefits they offer, but be very careful of switching careers because of all the dollar signs.

Keep repeating to yourself, "Money won't buy me happiness." Remember that you may make more money, but if you hate your new career, you'll probably be spending that money on stress- and health-related expenses. A career that's hot today could be gone tomorrow, so dig deeper if this is the only reason you want a new career.

If you have people in your life who are pressuring you to switch jobs, it can be very stressful, and you might be tempted to change careers just to "shut them up". Don't let your parents, significant others or anyone else influence your career choice. They don't have to live that career every day; you do.

If you love what you do and earn a reasonable living, why is it anyone's business but yours? If you switch careers because of outside pressure to have a "better career," and then hate your new career, you'll end up resenting whoever pressured you to make the switch.

It can be very helpful and even necessary for you to seek out the help of someone when making a career change. Having a mentor when you start this new career can be very valuable. As soon as you have identified the career field you want to switch into, begin developing new network contacts. Conduct informational interviews. Join industry associations.

People in your network can provide inside information about job-openings and can even champion you to hiring managers. Networking is essential for all job-seekers, but even more so for career-changers. And use a current or new mentor as a sounding board to help guide you in the transition.

Examine all possibilities before "diving in". Don't jump career fields without first conducting thorough research into all the possibilities, including career fields you may never have considered. By conducting research into careers you have never considered or been exposed to, you may find the career of your dreams.

Talk to people in your network, read career and job profiles; meet with a career management professional. The more information you have about various career choices, the more successful you'll be in making a career change.

Although we'll talk about this a little later, you really need to do some self-reflecting and really thinking about what you and what you don't like. Self-assessment of your skills, values, and interests is a critical component to career-change success. Make a list of the skills you love doing: in your job, in your hobbies, in all aspects of your life. Then list those things that you never want to do again.

You may want to consider taking one or more assessment tests, especially those with a career component. Preparing a SWOT (strengths, weaknesses, opportunities, threats) Analysis is also a useful activity. All these activities are designed so that you better understand yourself -- your product -- so that you can find the best career for you and then sell yourself to employers in that new career.

DO NOT change your career just because you've seen others succeed in that field. It's human nature to fall into the trap of comparing ourselves to others. Just because your best friend or neighbor is successful in a certain career does not mean that you will be -- or that you will be happy doing it -- so certainly consider the career field, but make sure you do the research before jumping into it.

Finally, just to add yet another cliché, too many job-seekers switch careers on the assumption that the grass is always greener -- and often times find out that is not the case.

You have to have some experience or education for almost all career fields. If you have neither for the field you want to get into, you'll most certainly fail. As a career-changer, you must find a way to bridge the experience, skills, and education gap between your old career and your new one.

While transferable skills – those that are applicable in multiple career fields, such as communications skills - are an important part of career change, it is often necessary to gain additional training and experience before you can find a good job in a new career field.

Research whether you need additional training, education, or certifications. And try to find time to volunteer, temp, intern, or consult in your new career field -- what some experts refer to as developing a parallel career -- before quitting your current job and searching for a full-time position in your new career field.

If you've been in your current position for quite some time, chances are good that a lot of things have changed in the job market since you were last out there. If you don't take the initiative to update your job skills – such as computer skills – then you won't enjoy as much success as you might want.

Review your resume-writing techniques, master networking, and polish your interviewing skills. What's the sense of doing all this research and preparation in attempting to change careers if you are not current with your job-search skills?

We mentioned a SWOT Analysis. This really is a useful tool when considering changing careers as well as in finding a job in general.

Let's look at how to construct your own SWOT Analysis.

Chapter 3

SWOT Analysis

(Return to Contents)

When speaking about a SWOT Analysis, this is a way of doing some serious self-reflecting and figuring out what your internal as well as external strengths and weaknesses are. Think of it as a pro and con list about you!

SWOT stands for strengths, weaknesses, opportunities, and threats. While we are hesitant to use the word "weakness" as it is very negative, using the word "shortcomings" doesn't make as catchy an acronym (SWOS) as SWOT!

Here are a few ideas when it comes to constructing your SWOT.

Internal Factors

Strengths - Internal positive aspects that are under control and upon which you may capitalize in planning for a new career. These would include:

- Work Experience
- Education, including value-added features
- Strong technical knowledge within your field (e.g. hardware, software, programming languages)
- Specific transferable skills (e.g., communication, teamwork, leadership skills)

- Personal characteristics (e.g., strong work ethic, self-discipline, ability to work under pressure, creativity, optimism, or a high level of energy)
- Good contacts/successful networking
- Interaction with professional organizations

Weaknesses - Internal negative aspects that are under your control and that you may plan to improve. These will include:

- Lack of Work Experience
- Low GPA, wrong major
- Lack of goals, lack of self-knowledge, lack of specific job knowledge
- Weak technical knowledge
- Weak skills (leadership, interpersonal, communication, teamwork)
- Weak job-hunting skills
- Negative personal characteristics (e.g., poor work ethic, lack of discipline, lack of motivation, indecisiveness, shyness, too emotional)

External Factors

Opportunities - Positive external conditions that you do not control but of which you can plan to take advantage. Here are some opportunities to list:

- Positive trends in your field that will create more jobs (e.g., growth, globalization, technological advances)
- Opportunities you could have in the field by enhancing your education
- Field is particularly in need of your set of skills

- Opportunities you could have through greater self-knowledge, more specific job goals
- Opportunities for advancement in your field
- Opportunities for professional development in your field
- Career path you've chosen provides unique opportunities
- Geography
- Strong network

Threats - Negative external conditions that you do not control but the effect of which you may be able to lessen. These include:

- Negative trends in your field that diminish jobs (downsizing, obsolescence)
- Competition from your cohort of college graduates
- Competitors with superior skills, experience, knowledge
- Competitors with better job-hunting skills than you
- Competitors who went to schools with better reputations.
- Obstacles in your way (e.g., lack of the advanced education/training you need to take advantage of opportunities)
- Limited advancement in your field, advancement is cut-throat and competitive
- Limited professional development in your field, so it's hard to stay marketable
- Companies are not hiring people with your major/degree

To further refine the SWOT, here are some other questions to ask about yourself:

Strengths:

- What are your advantages?
- What do you do well?
- Why did you decide to enter the field you will enter upon graduation?
- What were the motivating factors and influences?
- Do these factors still represent some of your inherent strengths?
- What need do you expect to fill within your organization?
- What have been your most notable achievements?
- To what do you attribute your success?
- How do you measure your success?
- What knowledge or expertise will you bring to the company you join that may not have been available to the organization before?
- What is your greatest asset?

Weaknesses:

- What could be improved?
- What do you do badly?
- What should you avoid?
- What are your professional weaknesses?
- How do they affect your job performance? (These might include weakness in technical skill areas or in leadership or interpersonal skills.)
- Think about your most unpleasant experiences in school or in past jobs and consider whether some aspect of your personal or professional life could be a root cause.

Opportunities:

- Where are the promising prospects facing you?
- What is the "state of the art" in your particular area of expertise?
- Are you doing everything you can to enhance your exposure to this area?
- What formal training and education can you add to your credentials that might position you appropriately for more opportunities?
- Would an MBA or another graduate degree add to your advantage?
- How quickly are you likely to advance in your chosen career?
- Useful opportunities can come from such things as:
- Changes in technology and markets on both a broad and industry-specific scale
- Changes in government policy related to your field
- Changes in social patterns, population profiles, lifestyle changes, etc.

Threats:
- What obstacles do you face?
- Are the requirements for your desired job field changing?
- Does changing technology threaten your prospective position?
- What is the current trend line for your personal area of expertise?
- Could your area of interest be fading in comparison with more emergent fields?
- Is your chosen field subject to internal politics that will lead to conflict?

- Is there any way to change the politics or to perhaps defuse your involvement in potential disputes?
- How might the economy negatively affect your future company and your work group?
- Will your future company provide enough access to new challenges to keep you sharp -- and marketable -- in the event of sudden unemployment?

Explore your own self-perception of your strengths, but also put yourself inside a prospective employer's head as you consider your strong points. Avoid false modesty, but also be brutally honest and realistic with yourself. Start out by simply making a list of words that describe you; chances are many of these characteristics compromise your strengths.

One of your greatest strengths can love the work you do. Learning to "follow your bliss" should be a critical component of managing your career. Some people know from an early age what kind of work will make them happy. For others, nailing down the self-knowledge that leads to career fulfillment comes from a process of exploring interests, skills, personality, learning style, and values.

In assessing your weaknesses, think about what prospective employers might consider to be the areas you could improve upon. Facing your frailties now can give you a huge head start in career planning.

As humans, we find it relatively difficult to identify the areas where we are weak. But this assessment helps to identify areas where we may need to improve. If you identify a skill that you know is in your chosen field, but you are weak in that skill area, you need to take steps to improve that skill. Past performance appraisals and even your grades and teacher comments from school provide valuable feedback.

Doing a SWOT will not only help to guide you toward a specific career that you will enjoy, it will also give you an idea of how to market yourself so that you can get that dream job that you want. From this analysis, you will have a road map that shows you how to capitalize on your strengths and minimize or eliminate your weaknesses. You should then use this map to take advantage of opportunities and avoid or lessen threats.

After you've analyzed your strengths, weaknesses, threats, and opportunities, you should use that information to plan how to market yourself.

The marketing planning process entails a three-step process:

1. Determining objectives

2. Developing marketing strategies

3. Strategizing an action program.

Objectives — define your career objectives. What is your ideal job upon graduation (or the job you would like to transition to from your current job)? What are some other positions you could accept? What is your five-year career goal?

Marketing Strategies — a broad marketing strategy or "game plan" for attaining your objectives. What are the companies and organizations you're going to target to obtain your objectives—your ideal job? How will you communicate with these firms? The strategies you identify should utilize all of the resources available to you, such as your personal network and a partnership with a mentor.

Action Programs — according to marketing principles, marketing strategies should be turned into specific action programs that answer a number of questions, including: What will be done? When will it be done? Who is responsible for doing it? Your key task here is setting specific timetables and deadlines for getting the career and company information you identified in the marketing strategy step.

So now that you've identified some key questions to ask when considering a career change, how do you know what the right career field is for you?

Chapter 4

Picking the Right Career Path

(Return to Contents)

For some people, finding the right job in an industry that excites you is an easy choice. When we're little, we always have an idea of what we want to be when we grow up. More often than not, we don't always get to realize that. As we grow older, not only do our interests change, but our realities change as well. The world can only have so many ballerinas, actresses, or professional ball players.

Therefore, facing the reality that you probably won't be doing what you thought you'd be doing back when you were eight years old can be a painful thought. However, some people do get to be what they always wanted to be. One man this writer knows had always dreamed of being a police officer. This can be a difficult field to get into and doesn't always happen overnight.

He knew that he'd have to work at it, but he also knew that he had to support his family. So he went to work in the family business and would test for the police department as openings were advertised. He could pass the tests, but would find himself in the lower part of the list that was compiled for possible new hires. For three years, he worked and waited.

Then, he had a successful tryout for one particular police department and found himself number two on the list. It just so happened that this particular force was hiring two officers and he was hired soon after. His dream had come true and he has had a successful career as a police officer and has received several awards for his police work.

Making a career change decision was easy for him. It was easy for this writer too.

Since I was little, all I've ever dreamed of doing was teaching. When I graduated from high school, my college major was education. I knew that I'd have to have extensive education if I was going to be a teacher, but I was committed to it and eagerly attended my classes with a goal in my mind.

Then, life changed. I suddenly found myself with two children, a husband who was also attending college, and bills piling up. My husband's part-time job just wasn't cutting it. It was decided that I would be the one to go to work since he was further along in school than I was. I took a job as a secretary and toiled away at similar jobs like that for six years.

I still took classes trying to work for my degree, but I was working full-time in jobs that I really didn't like. I found myself in the sales field eventually. While the money was terrific and I was good at selling, I still was unfulfilled. I would go to my children's parent-teacher conferences and find that longing to be a teacher still aching in the back of my mind as I spoke to their teachers and wandered the hallways of their school.

Then, life changed again. Only this time, it changed for the better. Our finances had finally reached the point where it would be possible for me to quit my job and attend school full-time to earn my bachelor's degree. It took two and a half years and some very hard work, but I was rewarded when I walked across the stage at my college and received my diploma with a Bachelor of Science degree in Elementary Education.

Now, I am a certified teacher – and a freelance writer – and am more satisfied now than I have ever been. While it was scary to make this drastic career change, it really was a no-brainer when it came to deciding what I wanted to do.

The point is that if you've always dreamed of working in a specific career field and it's possible for you to do so – even with a little hard work – go for your dreams and don't stop until you realize them.

For some people, however, a career change decision isn't as easy as mine was. They know they are unhappy in their current job and want to get out, but they really don't know what they want to do. Perhaps, also, they have a couple of ideas in their minds but are unsure as to which was to go.

High school graduates are also faced with an important decision when it comes to their career field. So many young people go to college taking core classes without knowing what they want their major to be.

So, are there certain things you need to consider when choosing a career field? In fact, there are many things that you need to keep in mind. You will want to be successful in whatever job field you choose, so it can be very important to be sure you are going to go into a business where you will be happy and where you can realize your full potential.

There are all sorts of tests you can take online that can help with your career field. What is a career test? It's a series of questions you answer based on what your preferences are or how you feel about specific job situations. The test will then analyze your answers and present you with the top jobs that fit you based on those answers. Some of the more accurate and reliable online career tests require you to purchase a membership or a package to get your results, but you can find some free career tests.

I took one test at www.livecareer.com and it was quite eye-opening. It was no surprise that the two job fields they recommended to me were writing and education! This website and test are free to users due to the sponsors that want you to sign up for information, so you do have to click through a lot of advertisements, but if you are not sure which career field you want to work in, this test can be a great place to start. Of course, you can "purchase" a more detailed and in-depth report at the end of the test which is what they want you to do, but that is strictly optional. I've found that most of the career testing sites will do this as well.

The basic format of many of these career tests are the same, for the most part. You are presented with three situations and you pick which one you prefer most and which one you prefer least. This is how they can find where your interests lie as well as where your abilities and talents can be best utilized.

Of course, when considering a career change or choice, you don't necessarily have to take a test. Take a look at what you enjoy doing. What have people said you are good at? Where could you be happiest? What are your interests and hobbies? You should also classify what's important to you and where you could make concessions.

For example, if spending time with your family is a priority, you probably won't want a job that requires extensive travel or overtime such as sales. If you are single or very career driven, you may want to look at a position that can provide for upward mobility when you put in hard work such as marketing or stocks.

What types of jobs are available to you? The choices are limitless and you will want to take a lot of things into consideration before you make the leap towards a career change.

Chapter 5

Opportunities Available To You

(Return to Contents)

Obviously, the choice of jobs is limitless as we need all sorts of people to perform all sorts of functions in society. Hotel clerks, salespeople, even the person at the drive-thru at McDonald's all serve important functions in life as we know it.

What one person may think of as a boring and mundane job might be another person's dream job, so there is a career out there that can fit good with you and your lifestyle and abilities.

Make a list of potential careers where you think you could be happy. Do you like helping people and think that social work would be a good fit for you? Maybe the medical field is more your speed. It's a good idea to simply identify the general field you want to work in and then explore the types of jobs that are available in that field.

We can't list every single option in this book due to space constraints, but here are a few career fields you may want to explore:

- Medicine/Health Care
- Sales
- Recreation
- Food Service

- Law Enforcement
- Education
- Social Work
- Marketing
- Performance
- Graphic Design
- Research
- Computers
- Outdoor Jobs
- Legal
- Sports
- Finance/Accounting
- Construction
- Child Care
- Service

Now, we'll narrow that list a little bit by giving you some ideas about jobs in these specific fields. Again, this is only a partial list and there are many, many other opportunities than just those listed here.

- Medicine/Health Care

Doctor, nurse, surgical technician, dentist, dental hygienist, dental assistant, phlebotomist, medical research, insurance specialist, x-ray technician, forensic scientist, coroner, physical therapist, pharmacist, pharmacy technician, hospice worker, elder care, MRI or CT technician, optometrist, mental health counselor, therapist, emergency medical technician, veterinarian, veterinary assistant, DNA profiler, and lab technician

- Sales

The possibilities in the sales field are endless and salespeople are always needed when a product is available for sale. Some possible sales jobs include yellow pages, radio, television, newspaper, pharmacy, medical equipment, office equipment, janitorial supplies, and food service supplies, telephone sales for various products, retail sales for various products, real estate, office supplies, industrial equipment, farm supplies, automobile sales, and insurance.

- Recreation

Park maintenance, coach, cruise director, dance instructor, karate instructor, travel agent, personal trainer, day camp director, amusement park personnel, managing a recreation complex, nursing home event coordinator, and tour guide

- Food Service

Cook/chef, sous chef, waiter/waitress, counter help at fast food restaurants, caterer, bus boy/girl, bartender, research cook, food critic, maitre 'd, hot dog vendor, nutritionist, dietician, menu planner for nursing homes and schools, recipe developer, winemaker, organic gardener, and lunch lady.

- Law Enforcement

Police officer, detective, dispatcher/telecommunicator, detective, crime scene investigator, private detective, evidence analyzer, prison guard, traffic cop, security guard, bail bondsman, bounty hunter, crime scene technician, and meter maid.

- Education

Teacher, teacher's aide, principal, superintendent, sales trainer, day care provider, pre-school teacher, test administrator, special education specialist, librarian, substitute teacher, English as a second language instructor, college professor, job placement coordinator, counselor, school nurse, and seminar director.

- Social Work

Welfare counselor, psychologist, child rights advocate, drug counselor, elderly rights advocate, nursing home administrator, adult day care provider, child abuse investigator, teacher for parenting classes, Lamaze instructor, hospice caregiver, therapist, and peer counselor

- Marketing

The marketing field is very similar to the sales field in that there are a myriad of possibilities available. Marketing and sales generally go hand in hand as they both are involved with promoting a product and generating income from the sales of that product. Nonetheless, here are a few marketing jobs to look at.

Public relations, advertising buyer, promotions director, advertising coordinator, brochure designer, celebrity agent, book agent, model agent, stylist, salesperson, advertising copywriter, commercial producer, and sales promotion

- Performance

Actor/actress, dancer, back-up singer, singer, ballerina, theater manager, set designer, musician, director, producer, playwright, screenwriter, camera operator, sound technician, recording studio manager, board operator, road assistant, costume designer, prop master, personal assistant, agent, cruise ship entertainer, comedian, casting director, dance instructor, commercial producer, and contract negotiator.

- Graphic Design

Logo development, yellow pages ad creator, brochure creator, layout artist, brand identity designer, creative/art director, illustrator, photo editor, multimedia designer in the film or television industry, photographer, web designer, and pre-press technician.

- Research

Biologist, scientist, medical researcher, pollster, agricultural research, fact checker, marketing researcher, field interviewer, statistician, and results coordinator.

- Computers

Computer programmer, video game designer, web site designer, computer repairman, software developer, data base programmer, key stroke technician, information technology coordinator, flash site designer, systems coordinator, LAN specialist, Internet specialist, systems engineer, network engineer, data entry, computer construction, troubleshooting specialist, and computer research.

- Outdoor Jobs

Lawn care, landscaper, zoologist, environmental engineer, outdoor adventure director, summer camp counselor, sky diving instructor, white water rafting guide, hiking guide, park ranger, fishing guide, campground administrator, ski instructor, organic farmer, tour guide, and botanist.

- Legal

Lawyer, paralegal, judge, court reporter, police officer, parole officer, legal secretary, politician, lobbyist, legal rights activist, mayor, council member, file clerk, adoption specialist, legal advisor, bankruptcy associate, contract administrator, court administrator, patent agent, law trainer, and legal trainer.

- Sports

Professional athlete, coach, referee, umpire, statistician, sports agent, sports instructor, team manager, weight trainer, sports marketing, equipment manager, promotions, director of sports relations, ticket agent, talent scout, stadium manager, scheduler, sponsorship coordinator, and team development.

- Finance/Accounting

Certified public accountant, bookkeeper, banker, stock broker, market analyst, mortgage specialist, bank teller, auditor, tax accountant, controller, tax preparer, budget analyst, loan officer, commodities broker, insurance underwriter, financial manager, insurance adjuster, insurance investigator, insurance examiner, collections agent, and investment banker.

- Construction

Carpenter, dry wall hanger, electrician, plumber, architect, roofer, carpet installer, tile layer, engineer, estimator, civil engineer, paver, project coordinator, surveyor, heavy equipment operator, safety coordinator, painter, gutter installer, septic system installer, deck builder, and project foreman.

- Service

Wedding planner, event coordinator, advertising specialty item creator, house cleaner, lawn care, tree trimmer, garbage person, closet organizer, home inventory specialist, photographer, dee jay, floral designer, life coach, street sweeper, handyman, car detailer, antique dealer, thrift shop manager, assistant to the elderly, clothing designer, interior decorator, and budget advisor.

Of course, the list above is merely a sampling of what kinds of jobs you can look for. Keep in mind that all industries and job fields need clerical help like secretaries, file clerks, and receptionists. Almost all fields also need sales people and marketing specialists as well as computer advisors and troubleshooters. Starting out in jobs like this can be a great way to move up in a specific job industry with experience.

The thing about making a career change is that you want to work in a job that fits well with you and your personality. You want it to be interesting to you and that you look forward to going to work instead of dreading it.

Many jobs will require additional education or some type of training. If you have always wanted to be an attorney, you'll have to go to law school – obviously. But remember that you are not happy with your present job and want to work in the legal field.

Register for law school and apply for a job with a firm that can help you in the future and learn more about the business such as a legal secretary or even a paralegal.

When you consider that you are trying to better yourself and make yourself happier, the extra education will be well worth it. There's nothing more satisfying than knowing you've worked hard to get into an industry where you'll be happy working. It's a fulfilling journey, believe me!

You may be curious to know what the hottest jobs are right now. Maybe one of them will interest you!

Chapter 6

Hot Jobs

(Return to Contents)

Trends Magazine has compiled a list of the hottest new jobs for the twenty-first century. Most of them are hot because of emerging technologies and the need for people who know about those new technologies. These jobs can be very lucrative to the person who is lucky enough to secure employment in these areas. Here they are:

- Experience Designer: These individuals work in the retail industry, creating the essence and aura of a store. Experience designers go beyond the look of a place, creating a unique experience in which shoppers can immerse themselves. From cellular boutiques to the American Girl doll store on New York's Fifth Avenue, the shops created by an experience designer are often considered works of art; mini universes unto themselves.

Experience designers are involved in every aspect of creation -- from choosing accent colors on walls to slanting the windows in the right direction. The next time you go into a boutique and you feel as if you've just had an "experience" -- you have, and someone went to a lot of trouble to make you feel at home.

- Medical Researcher: It's no news that what's on the forefront of medicine is on the forefront of America's collective mind. Researchers of cancer, Alzheimer's, and the developers of prosthetics are the most coveted titles in the healthcare industry.

With the aging baby boomer population, the need for cures and treatment plans is both paramount and profitable.

Major developments aren't only taking place in medicine, but also in the way doctors file medical records. Individuals with the know-how and creative juice to mix tech with medicine can expect seven figure salaries in the year ahead.

- Web Designer: What's new about web designers? We already know they have cool jobs, working as the creative arm behind highly trafficked websites. But Trendsresearch.com reports that the profession is still in its adolescent phase, and for 2007 it's going to be a new era of web design. Monster.com charts a 26 percent growth rate in this field for the past year, which will continue to blossom for the coming year.

With the advent of new flash technology, companies are looking for people who know how to implement this into their web presence since so many people rely on the Internet for information. Being a web designer is definitely one of the hottest jobs around and some companies will also let you work from home!

- Security Systems Engineer: Monster.com reports that individuals in the protective services industry can expect a rise in demand and salary for 2007. Advances in Vegas-Casino like security systems and satellite maps are helping to wire the world for defense.

Individuals with a head for engineering and computers can easily expect a six-figure salary in this industry. From sonar imaging to keystroke identification, keeping our country and our world safer has never been easier or more profitable.

- Urban Planners: From the Hong Kong International Airport Residential Tower to suburban "McMansion" sprawl, individuals in residential planning and development can expect a lot of work in the coming year. Urban Planners must meet the demand for real estate that's both decadent and practical. Prefab one-level homes engineered for the aging baby boomer population are changing the face of suburban America, and boosting the demand for urban planners.

- Viral Marketers and Media Promoters: Not to be confused with someone in advertising or public relations, a viral marketer knows how to build an audience from nothing with little more than rumor and excitement. Known for such coups as My Space's Lonelygirl15 and the Blair Witch Project, Viral Marketers begin "contagious" campaigns that spread largely through word of mouth. They now have a foothold in American advertising due largely to the Internet.

- Talent Agents: As Clint Eastwood would say, "These days, everyone is famous." And as fame and fortune grows for performers and athletes, a new arena opens for their managers, promoters, and general go-to guys.

Although these titles may speak for themselves, duties for those fortunate enough to get close to the stars often include things like latte retrieval and limo reservations. Yet, next to the celebrities themselves, these positions are some of the most competitive in the entertainment industry as well as in the most demand.

- Buyers and purchasing agents: Trend forecasters predict that 2007 could be a make-or-break year for the retail industry, specifically the department store. Much of the department store's fate lies in the hands of the buyers and purchasing agents.

These individuals are in charge of store inventory and make decisions on item color, size, quantity, and country of origin. With the recent boom of the retail industry, these jobs are often hard to come by and can be very lucrative if store profitability increases.

- Art Directors: From Broadway to movie sets, any job that involves paint, lights, cameras, and action is in demand, especially within the 20-30 demographic. Now perceived as the ultimate career for inspired artists with an affinity for pop culture, art directors, set directors, and stage production directors clamor for the top positions that call for hands-on creative genius with a couture designer's eye.

- News Analysts, Reporters, and Bloggers: The Internet has created a new realm for reporters and writers, who previously only saw their names and ideas in print. Now, publications with an online division often hire three levels of correspondents: print news writers, online news writers, and bloggers.

Although most personal blogs aren't profitable enough to stand alone as businesses, writers can use their increasing popularity as another gateway for their voices to be heard.

There is also a list of jobs that are in the biggest demand these days compiled by the folks at CNN Money. There is high demand for workers in the following fields:

- Accounting - Thanks to Enron and the Sarbanes-Oxley Act of 2002, those who have a few years of corporate auditing experience working for a large public accounting firm can negotiate a sweet package for themselves when they change jobs.

That applies whether they're leaving the accounting firm to go work for a corporation or if they're seeking to return to the public accounting firm from an auditing job at an individual company. College graduates with an accounting degree but not yet a CPA designation might make between $35,000 and $45,000 a year, or up to $50,000 in large cities like New York. After a couple of years they can command a substantial pay hike if they move to large company as an internal staff auditor or to a smaller company as controller. At that point, their salary can jump to anywhere from $50,000 to $75,000.

The expectation is that they will obtain their CPA designation.

If they choose to return to a public accounting firm as an audit manager after a couple of years at a corporation they can earn a salary of $70,000 to $85,000.

- Sales and Marketing - The healthcare and biomedical fields offer some handsome earnings opportunities for those on the business side.

Business development directors, product managers and associate product managers working for medical device makers, for instance, can do quite well for themselves if they develop a successful track record managing the concept, execution and sales strategy for a medical device before jumping ship.

Typically, they have an MBA in marketing plus at least two to three years' experience on the junior end to between five and eight years' experience at the more senior levels. That experience ideally will be in the industry where they're seeking work.

An associate product manager might make a base salary of $55,000 to $75,000. A product manager can make a base of $75,000 to $95,000, while a business development director may make $120,000 to $160,000. Those salaries don't include bonuses. The business development director seeking a vice president position could boost his base to $150,000 to $200,000 -- depending on whether the new company is a risky start-up or established device maker.

- Legal - Intellectual property attorneys specializing in patent law and the legal secretaries who have experience helping to prepare patent applications are highly desirable these days.

The most in demand are those lawyers with not only a J.D. but also an advanced degree in electrical and mechanical engineering, chemical engineering, biotechnology, pharmacology or computer science. Even those patent lawyers who just have an undergraduate degree in those fields have a leg up.

Patent lawyers working for a law firm might make $125,000 to $135,000 to start or about $90,000 if they work for a corporation that's trying to get a patent or to protect one they already have. With a couple of years' experience, they can expect a 10 percent jump or better when they get another job.

Legal secretaries, meanwhile, might make $65,000 at a law firm or $55,000 at a corporation. Should they choose to move to a new employer, they can command close to a 10 percent bump in pay.

- Technology - Two tech jobs in high demand these days are .NET (dot net) developers and quality assurance analysts.

Developers who are expert users of Microsoft's software programming language .NET can make between $75,000 and $85,000 a year in major cities. If they pursue a job at a company that seeks someone with a background in a given field (say, a firm looking for a .NET developer experienced in using software related to derivatives) they might snag a salary hike of 15 percent or more when they switch jobs.

Those who work in software quality management, meanwhile, might make $65,000 to $75,000 a year and be able to negotiate a 10 percent to 15 percent jump in pay if they switch jobs.

- Manufacturing and Engineering - Despite all the announced job cuts in the automotive industry, quality and process engineers, as well as plant managers certified in what's known as "Lean Manufacturing" techniques, are hot commodities.

The same applies to professionals in similar positions at other types of manufacturers.

One lean manufacturing technique is to use video cameras to capture the manufacturing process. A quality engineer will analyze the tapes to identify areas in the process that create inefficiencies or excess waste, both in terms of materials and workers' time.

Process and manufacturing engineers might make between $65,000 and $75,000. With a certification in lean manufacturing and a few years' experience, they can command pay hikes of between 15 percent and 20 percent if they choose to switch jobs. A plant manager making between $90,000 and $120,000 may expect to get a 10 percent raise or more. Many of the salaries quoted here are based on working in larger cities as opposed to smaller towns; however, it is certainly possible to garner wages such as these when you are working in an industry where there are shortages of knowledgeable individuals. There's no question that these job fields are lucrative and need workers that can not only perform the job, but do it well.

What about the fastest growing jobs in America? Here they are separated according to your level of education:

High School Diploma or GED

Home Health Aide

Home health aides provide services to the elderly, people with disabilities, and those who are ill, that allow them to live at home. Employment of home health aides is projected to grow by 56% between 2006 and 2014. Median hourly earnings were over $10 in 2004.

Medical Assistant

Medical assistants perform administrative duties in physicians' offices. They may also perform some clinical duties as allowed by individual state laws. Employment in this field is expected to grow by 52% between 2004 and 2014. Medical assistants' median hourly wages were just over $12 in 2006.

Dental Assistant

Dental assistants perform duties that may include patient care, laboratory work, and office work. There is expected to be a 43%

growth in employment between 2006 and 2014. Dental assistants earned a median hourly wage of $13.62 in 2006.

Personal and Home Care Aide

Personal and home care aides provide housekeeping and routine personal care services to those who are elderly, disabled, ill, or mentally disabled allowing them to remain in their own homes. We can expect to see a 41% increase in the employment of personal and home care aides between 2006 and 2014. Median hourly earnings for those working in this field were $8.12 in 2006.

Physical Therapist Aide

Physical therapist aides keep treatment areas clean, prepare for each patient's session, and help patients get to or from treatment areas. Employment in this field is expected to grow by 34% between 2006 and 2014. Median hourly earnings of physical therapist aides were $10.28 in 2006.

Hazardous Materials Removal Worker

Hazardous materials removal workers identify, remove, package, and transport hazardous materials (hazmats). There is expected to be a 31% increase in employment in this field between 2006 and 2014. Hazmat removal workers' median hourly wage, at $16.02 as of 2006, is the highest on this list.

Social And Human Service Assistant

Social and human service assistant is a generic term that encompasses job titles including human service workers, case management aides, social work assistants, community support workers, mental health aides, community outreach workers, life skill counselors, and gerontology aides. Employment of social and human service assistants is expected to increase by 30% between 2006 and 2014. Median hourly earnings were $11.89 in 2006.

Residential Advisor

Residential advisors coordinate the activities of those living in boarding schools, college dormitories, or sorority and fraternity houses. Employment of residential advisors is expected to grow by 29% between 2006 and 2014. The median hourly wages were $10.47 in 2006.

Pharmacy Technician

Pharmacy technicians assist pharmacists by counting tablets, labeling bottles, and performing other routine tasks. We can expect to see a 29% growth in employment between 2006 and 2014. The median hourly wages of pharmacy technicians were $11.37 in 2006.

Ambulance Driver and Attendant

Ambulance drivers and attendants transport sick or injured people and assist in lifting patients. This occupation is not to be confused with emergency medical technician. There is expected to be a 29% increase in employment of ambulance drivers and attendants. Median hourly earnings were $9.31 in 2006.

Bachelor's Degree

Network Systems and Data Communications Analyst

Network systems and data communications analysts design and evaluate network systems, for example, local area networks (LANs), Wide Area Networks (WANs), and Internet systems. Employment of network systems and data communications analysts is projected to grow by 55% through 2014. Median annual earnings were $61,300 in 2006 and median hourly earnings were $29.45.

Physician Assistant

Physician assistants (PAs) perform diagnostic, therapeutic, and preventive health care services under the supervision of physicians. Employment in this field is expected to grow by 50% through 2014.

Physician assistants' median annual salaries were $69,200 in 2006 and hourly wages were $33.29.

Computer Applications Software Engineer

Computer applications software engineers use different programming languages to design, construct, and maintain software along with specialized utility programs. They analyze users' needs in order to do this. There is expected to be a 48% growth in employment through 2014. Computer applications software engineers earned a median annual salary of $76,300 and an hourly wage of $36.69 in 2006.

Computer Systems Software Engineer

Computer systems software engineers build and maintain companies' computer systems and plan their future growth. We can expect to see a 43% increase in the employment of computer systems software engineers through 2014. The median annual salary was $81,100 in 2006 and the median hourly earnings were slightly over $39.

Network and Computer Systems Administrator

Network and computer systems administrators maintain and monitor computer systems. Those with experience take on more responsibilities which include making recommendations about the company network to management. Employment in this field is expected to grow by 38% through 2014. Network and computer systems administrators earned an annual salary of $59,100 in 2006 and hourly wages of $28.42.

Database Administrator

Database administrators determine ways to organize and store data, working with database management systems software. There is expected to be a 38% increase in employment in this field through

2014. Database administrators earned an annual salary of $61,900 in 2006 and median hourly wages of $29.78.

Computer Systems Analyst

Computer systems analysts use computer technology to meet the needs of their employers. They also solve computer problems. Employment of computer systems analysts is expected to increase by 31% through 2014. Median annual earnings were $67,500 in 2006 and median hourly wages were $32.46.

Biomedical Engineer

Biomedical engineers use their knowledge of biology and medicine, combined with engineering practices and principles, to develop devices and procedures that solve medical and health-related problems. Employment in this field is expected to grow by 31% through 2014. The median annual salary was $70,500 in 2006 and median hourly wages were $33.90.

Employment, Recruitment and Placement Specialist

Employment, recruitment and placement specialists are responsible for hiring new employees. We can expect to see a 30% growth in employment through 2014. The median annual salary of employment, recruitment and placement specialists was $41,200 in 2006 and median hourly wages were $19.80.

Environmental Engineer

Environmental engineers use the principles of biology and chemistry to develop solutions to environmental problems. There is expected to be a 30% increase in employment in this field. Median annual earnings of environmental engineers were $67,600 in 2006 and median hourly wages were $32.51.

Master's or Doctorate

Physical Therapist

Physical therapists (PTs) provide services that restore patients' functions, improve mobility, relieve pain, and prevent or limit permanent physical disabilities. Employment of physical therapists is expected grow by 37% through Median annual earnings were $61,600 in 2006. Median hourly earnings were $29.60.

Medical Scientist (Except Epidemiologist)

Medical scientists (except epidemiologists) generally have master's degrees. They conduct research about human diseases, but do not practice medicine. Employment of medical scientists (except epidemiologists) is expected to grow by 34% between 2006 and 2014. The median annual salary in this field was $60,200 in 2006. The median hourly salary in that year was just over $21.

Occupational Therapist

Occupational therapists (OTs) help people who have disabling conditions improve their ability to perform tasks in their daily living and working environments. There is expected to be a 34% growth in employment of occupational therapists between 2006 and 2014. Occupational therapists earned a median annual salary of $55,600 in 2006 and a median hourly wage of $26.75.

Postsecondary Teacher

Postsecondary teachers instruct students above the high school level. They work in colleges, universities, and career, trade and technical schools. Included are faculty members and graduate assistants. Employment of postsecondary teachers is expected to see a 32% increase through 2014. Median yearly earnings in this field are $51,800 and vary by rank, field of study, type of institution, and geographic area.

Hydrologist

Hydrologists study the quantity, distribution, circulation, and physical properties of underground and surface waters. Employment in this field is expected to grow by 32% through 2014. Median annual earnings of hydrologists were $60,900 in 2004. Median hourly earnings were $29.27.

Substance Abuse and Behavioral Disorder Counselor

Substance abuse and behavioral disorder counselors help those who have problems with drug, alcohol and gambling addictions and with eating disorders. There is expected to be a 29% increase in employment in this field through 2014. Substance abuse and behavioral disorder counselors earned a median annual salary of $32,600 or a median hourly wage of $15.69 in 2006.

Instructional Coordinator

An instructional coordinator's job is to improve the quality of education in the classroom. Instructional coordinators also are called curriculum specialists, staff development specialists, or directors of instructional material. Employment in this field is expected to increase by 28% through 2014. Median annual earnings were $50,100 in 2006. Median hourly wages were just over $24.

Mental Health Counselor

Mental health counselors address and treat mental and emotional disorders and promote optimum mental health. Employment of mental health counselors is expected to grow by 27% through 2014. The median annual salary was $33,400 in 2006 and the median hourly wage was just over $16.

Mental Health and Substance Abuse Social Worker

Mental health and substance abuse social workers provide individual and group therapy, outreach, crisis intervention, social rehabilitation, and training in skills of everyday living to those with substance abuse issues. We can expect to see a 27% growth in employment through 2014. The median annual salary was $34,300 in 2006 and median hourly wages were $16.50.

Epidemiologist

Epidemiologists investigate and describe the determinants of disease, disability, and other health outcomes and develop the means for prevention and control. There is expected to be a 26% increase in employment of epidemiologists. Median annual earnings were $52,500 in 2006. Median hourly wages were $25.25.

Finally, we have the list of jobs with the most vacancies. That means your chance of finding employment in these areas is very good.

Retail Salesperson

Retail salespeople assist customers. They receive most of their training on the job. The median hourly earnings of retail salespersons were $8.98 in May 2006. That figure includes commissions. The starting hourly wage for salespeople is generally the minimum wage. Nationally that wage is $5.15 an hour, but it may vary by state.

Cashier

Cashiers work in supermarkets, department stores, gas stations, movie theaters, as well as in other businesses. They usually receive short-term on-the-job training. A cashier earns a median hourly wage of $7.81, but most start off earning the minimum wage. The Federal minimum wage is $5.15 per hour but it may vary by state.

Waiter and Waitress

Waiters and waitresses serve food and beverages to restaurant clientele. They receive short-term on-the-job training. The median hourly wage for waiters and waitresses is $6.75 (as of May 2006), which includes tips. Tips usually range from 10% to 20% of the total bill and are usually given at the customer's discretion.

Food Preparation And Serving Workers (including fast food)

Most food preparation workers receive short-term on-the-job training. Executive chefs and those who work in fine restaurants usually receive much more extensive training. Earnings vary greatly by type of job and by location. The median hourly earnings for food preparation workers were $8.03 in May 2006.

Registered Nurse

Most registered nurses providing direct patient care in hospitals. A registered nurse must have a bachelor's of science degree in nursing, an associate degree in nursing, or a diploma issued by a hospital. Median annual earnings of registered nurses were $52,330 in May 2006. This is one of the highest paying occupations on this list, and also requires more training than all but one other occupation.

Laborers and Hand Material Movers

Laborers and hand material movers manually move freight, stock and other materials. They receive short-term on-the-job training. Laborers and hand material movers earned a median hourly rate of $9.67 in 2006.

General Office Clerk

General office clerks carry out various duties which may change on a daily basis. They receive short-term on-the-job training. Median annual earnings for general office clerks were $22,770 in 2006.

Postsecondary Teachers

Postsecondary teachers include college and university faculty, postsecondary career and technical education teachers, and graduate teaching assistants. Education and training requirements for postsecondary teachers are the highest of all occupations on this list, ranging from a bachelor's degree to a doctorate degree.

The median earnings for those in this occupation were also higher than for others on this list. They were $51,800 in 2006, but vary according to position and level of education.

Janitors and Cleaners (except maids and housekeeping cleaners)

Janitors and cleaners perform heavy cleaning duties. They receive short-term on-the-job training. Their median annual earnings were $18,790 in 2006.

Customer Service Representatives

Customer service representatives help customers with their questions and concerns. They receive moderate on-the-job training. Median annual earnings of customer service representatives in 2006 were $27,020.

Now that you have so many options open to you, it's time to really explore making your career change.

Chapter 7

What Comes Next

(Return to Contents)

It's essential that you do your research before you jump in head first towards a new career path. Once you have your list of possible jobs narrowed down, you'll need to look at the requirements it takes to do the job. Will you need more education or training? Are there jobs in this field available in your area? Can you support your family on what the expected wages are going to be?

You will also want to know what to expect when you are considering a career change to a different field than what you're working in now. This is where an informational interview can be very helpful. The purpose of an informational interview is to get information about a field of work from someone who has some firsthand knowledge.

You can do an informational interview in a couple of different ways. You could talk informally to someone you know who is doing similar work. Ask friends, relatives, fellow students, your teachers, and neighbors if they know someone who works in your targeted field. People love to talk about themselves and what they do, so you can find out some valuable information just by having lunch or dinner with someone who has your "dream job".

You can also contact a company in the field you are considering and ask the human resources director if you could set an appointment with them to talk about the jobs available and what they entail. This serves a dual purpose. First, you will be making contacts in the business you are interested in. Once you get the necessary education and training and you are ready to ask for a job, chances are good that they will remember you and that will get you an "in".

Asking for an informational interview like this also shows that you are a thorough person who takes the time to do research and find out information about a specific career path. People in the business field talk to each other all the time. Networking is an important part of almost every job.

The old saying "It's who you know" is true and it can make a difference if filling a job comes down to you and another person. It can get you the edge you need to get hired.

When you are doing a formal informational interview, you will want to go into it prepared. There's nothing worse than looking less than intelligent and unprepared when a human resources manager has agreed to take the time to talk with you. You should have a list of questions ready when you walk through the door. Here is a sampling of some things you might want to ask:

- Describe a typical day at work.
- How many hours do you normally work in a week?
- What do you see as the potential for growth in this field?
- What can I do now to help me find employment in this field?
- Are there any educational requirements for this job such as a specific degree, etc.?

Whatever you do, DO NOT ask for a job when you are doing an informational interview. When you called, you asked to speak with the human resources person, your purpose was to simply gather information for yourself and that is what they will be prepared for. There's plenty of time to submit your resume later. This is just an educational mission, not a job interview. Just as with a real job interview, it's important to make a good impression – especially if you have aspirations toward working for that specific company. Dress appropriately, arrive early, keep your questions short and concise, don't take up too much of the person's time, and remember the basic rules of etiquette. Since they may be the one hiring you someday, you will want them to remember you in a positive light.

Because making a career change is so important and a very big step, it's also important for you to have an action plan. In the above chapter about things not to do when making a career change, we mentioned that you should have a plan as to how you will be going about this life-changing event. It helps if you begin by setting some goals and then devising an action plan.

A goal is something that you want to achieve. It is the end result of what might be a lot of hard work but that hard work will help you realize your dream of working in a job that you'll love.

There are two types of goals you need to set: long-term and short-term. Long term goals can take about three to five years to achieve. Short term goals can be realized within a year or so. It's important to have goals because you need to have something to focus on – keeping your eye on the prize so to speak! When you are setting goals, you need to keep in mind a few things. Your goals should be:

- conceivable: you must be able to put it into words;
- achievable: you must have the attributes, energy, and time to accomplish it;
- believable: you must believe you can reach it;
- achievable within a certain time frame: you must be able to state how long it will take you to reach it;
- clearly defined: you must know exactly what it is;
- flexible: you must be willing to modify it as necessary;

Once you have your goals set, you can move on to making a career action plan. This will list all of your goals along with the steps you have to take to realize your goals. Having all of this information written down will make it more real and motivate you to achieve those goals and realize success.

A career action plan is a road map that takes you from choosing an occupation to becoming employed in that occupation to reaching your long-term career goals. The career planning process is ongoing, and bi-directional, meaning you can move back to previous steps when you need to gather more information or clarify your choices. Once you have identified an occupation to pursue you should develop an action plan.

According to Individualized Career Plan Models - Eric Digest No. 71(ERIC Clearinghouse on Adult Career and Vocational Education), "Personal plans of action -- individualized career development plans -- are becoming important instruments that counselors and others are using to help their students and/or clients (both youth and adults) meet their changing goals, interests and needs in this fast-paced, rapidly changing society."

Though the ERIC Digest talks about individualized career plans being used by counselors and other professionals, you can develop a plan yourself. Even if you do work with a counselor, you will need to do some of the work yourself.

For example, a counselor can't set your goals for you. He or she will just help you clarify your goals and help you find strategies to reach them. In addition, an action plan should be amended over time as your goals change, your priorities change, and your career grows. Let's begin now to take a look at how to develop a career action plan step-by-step.Begin your career action plan by writing down your educational background and employment history. When you are listing previous jobs, start with the most recent one first and work your way back. Include the location of the company, your job title, and the dates you worked at that job. When you put together your resume, having organized this information will prove very helpful.

Then you will want to outline your education and training. Again, start with the most recent and work your way into the past. List the schools you've attended, the dates you've attended them, and the credits, certificates, or degrees you've earned. Also list additional training and any professional licenses you hold. You should also list volunteer or other unpaid experience.

You may find that several of these activities are relevant to your occupational goals. By volunteering you may have developed skills that will play an important role in your future career. Again, this information can be used on your resume. It can also be used in job interviews, or when applying to college or graduate school.

If during the career planning process you met with a career development professional that used self assessment tools to help you gather information about yourself, this is where you can write down the results of those assessments. If you took one of the online career assessment tests, this is where you want to put the results as well.

You can then list the occupations that were suggested to you during that phase. You may even want to attach the information you gathered when you explored those occupations in case you want to refer to your notes later on.

Out of all the occupations you explored, at some point in the process you narrowed your choices down to one occupation. That is the one you plan to you took one of the online career assessment tests, this is where you want to put the results as well.

You can then list the occupations that were suggested to you during that phase. You may even want to attach the information you gathered when you explored those occupations in case you want to refer to your notes later on.

Out of all the occupations you explored, at some point in the process you narrowed your choices down to one occupation. That is the one you plan to pursue. You may even have two occupations -- one to pursue in the short term and one to pursue in the long term.

They should be related, the second being one that is a step up from the first. For example, you can say you want to first become a nurse's aide, and then after you get some experience you will pursue a career as a registered nurse.

You should break your career plan down into goals you can reach in a year or less and goals you want to reach in five years or less. You can use increments of one or two years in this five year plan as well. This breakdown will make your plan easier for you to follow.

You should also include your goals for education and training. Your occupational goals and your educational goals should correspond to one another, since reaching your occupational goals will usually be dependent upon reaching your educational goals.

If your long term occupational goal is to be a lawyer, here's what your short and long term plans might look like:

- Year One: Complete my bachelor's degree (12 credits left to go), apply to law school, get accepted to law school (a positive attitude is a good thing)
- Year Two through Year Four: Enter law school, study hard and earn good grades, graduate from law school with many job offers
- Year Five: Begin working in a law firm

You are likely to encounter barriers along the way to realizing your goals. This is normal and to be expected. You will have a better chance of overcoming those barriers and obstacles if you try to ascertain what they might be and then come up with a plan to defeat them if they do arise.

For example you may be the primary caregiver for your children or elderly parents. This may interfere with your ability to complete your degree. You can deal with this barrier by enlisting the help of your spouse or another relative. Perhaps you can arrange for child or adult daycare.

Some might say that going through so many steps just to choose a career is wasting time and doesn't serve any purpose, but nothing could be further from the truth. A well-thought-out career action plan will prove to be a very useful tool.

You've gone through the career planning process carefully choosing a suitable occupation. Setting goals and planning what you need to do to realize them will insure that you reach your career destination.

So you've got a career action plan and it's time for you to quit your present job. You'll want to do this in the right way.

Chapter 8

Saying Goodbye To Your Job

(Return to Contents)

In the business world, it's important that you remember not to burn any bridges. Even if you absolutely HATE your job, where you work, your co-workers, or your boss, you should still conduct yourself in a professional manner when you leave. Doing so will show everyone how much class and integrity you have and it will be remembered!

When you leave your job, your emotions may be running high, especially if you are leaving on bad terms. You may want to tell your boss or co-workers what you really think of them. Don't do it, even if they truly deserve it. You never know who you will meet down the road and who you may have to work with one day.

Don't damage company property or steal something when you leave. You may feel you were mistreated by your employer and you may be really angry. However, vandalism and theft are criminal offenses. Not only will your professional reputation be damaged by your actions, you could end up in jail.

Be sure to ask for a reference or a letter of recommendation. This may sound like an odd thing to consider if you are leaving your job on unfavorable terms. However, you will have to include this job on your resume, so you should try to make sure you get either a good or, at least, a neutral reference.

If you've been fired because of some horrible offense, this may be a moot point. However if your parting is due to something less serious, you may be able to ask your boss for a reference, in spite of the fact that "things didn't work out as expected."

If your company has hired a replacement for your job and you have the opportunity to be around him or her, do not badmouth your boss, your co-workers, or the company in general. First of all, it will only look like sour grapes, so there's nothing to gain here. Second, your successor will figure things out for himself or herself.

Third, it may have been bad chemistry, and your co-worker will have a totally different experience than you did.

When you are ready to start interviewing, it's also important to remember the above suggestion: don't bad mouth the company or your boss. The only person who this will make look bad is you. Your prospective boss will wonder what caused your relationship with your prior employer to sour and will suspect that you could have been at fault.

Once you've decided to leave, you'll want to put your intentions in writing so that it can go into your personnel file. This is good manners as well and let's you tell your Dear Mr. Smith

The purpose of this letter is to inform you that, effective May 31, I will be leaving my position with the company. I have decided to take a new career path and work in a different industry. That will require me to obtain further education, and I plan to be in school full-time beginning with the summer term. My time here has been enjoyable and I hope my work has been satisfactory. I would appreciate it if you would provide me with a good reference when the time comes for me to begin job hunting. Thank you so much for everything.

Sincerely,

(You)

Here is another sample letter:

Dear Mr. Smith:

Please be advised that effective May 31, I will be leaving my position with the company. I have secured employment elsewhere that is a better fit for my life as well as my goals. I will be happy to train a replacement should you find one before my ending date.

I hope I can count on you for a positive reference if needed in the future and thank you for the opportunity to work for you.

Sincerely,

(You)

The standard time frame to give notice is a minimum of two weeks prior to your intended quit date. However, it's often nice to give your employer as much time as possible to find a replacement for you. If you signed a contract with your employer, check the terms to see if you are required to give notice for a specific time frame. Otherwise, two weeks is the norm.

If your employer asks you stay longer than two weeks (or the time period in your contract) you have no obligation to stay. Your new employer will be expecting you to start as scheduled, and in a timely manner. What you could do, is offer to help your previous employer, if necessary, after hours, via email or on the phone.

Don't say much more than you are leaving. Emphasize the positive and talk about how the company has benefited you, but, mention that it's time to move on. You can offer to help during the transition and afterwards. Don't be negative. There's no point - you're leaving and you want to leave on good terms.

You may want to tell your co-workers that you're leaving – especially if you've made friends there. But, don't tell anyone else until you've told your boss. You don't want the news to leak out before you're ready and it's just in poor form for your boss to find out from someone other than you.

Another huge part of making a career change is finding a new job once you've satisfied educational requirements and how to land that job.

Chapter 9

Finding and Getting That New Job

(Return to Contents)

After you've decided what it is that you REALLY want to do with you life and you have the education you need, now's the time to go out and get that new job and get well on your way to a new and exciting career. Luckily, it's not as difficult as it might seem!

You literally have hundreds and hundreds of resources at your fingertips when it comes to the job hunt! If you are willing to relocate, your options are multiplied, but even if you want to stay put, you can either face commuting or even find something right where you live.

Start by looking in your local newspaper as well as papers from the towns surrounding you. Employers generally concentrate on the weekend editions of the papers to advertise job openings – especially the Sunday paper. You'll be able to see what's available out there and narrow down your search based on these ads.

Another great resource is the Internet. We live in the Information Age, and there are many, many websites dedicated to the job seeker. These sites allow you to post your resume online and to search available jobs all over the country and even all over the world.

When I was looking for a sales job, I posted my resume on monster.com and had a phone call within an hour of posting, so these websites can be extremely valuable to the job seeker. Here are some of the more popular sites:

- www.monster.com
- www.career.com
- www.job.com
- www.yahoohotjobs.com
- www.careerbuilder.com

Your Resume

Once you've found a job you are interested in, it's time to submit your resume. Here are some valuable tips on creating your resume for the best impression.

- Your name and contact information should appear at the top of the page with your name being larger than the rest of the typestyle. Include your physical address, your home phone, your cell phone, and your e-mail address.

- If you are making a career change, the next section should list your job experience starting with your most recent job and working backwards. Then you follow up with your education. If you are a new graduate, start your resume listing your education including degrees earned and any honors you achieved and follow it with any jobs you've worked in the next section.

- You will want to have a section that lists any special talents you have (that pertain to the job) and things like software programs you can use, office machines you can operate, etc.

- Be sure to list any organizations you belong to and any honors that have been bestowed upon you. Employers like to see people who are involved in activities outside of work.

- The very last section will be for references. In almost all cases, you should state on your resume that "References are available upon request." When you get the interview is when you should present them with your reference list.

- Consider printing your resume on demurely colored paper. I've used a light green marble, cream, even blue tinted paper. This makes your resume stand out in a stack of white paper and increases your chance to have your resume noticed first. The paper should be heavier than regular paper as well. Generally, a 20# paper is best to use.

- It's almost always best to take your resume to the prospective employer in person and ask to speak with the person doing the hiring. You want to get as much exposure as you possibly can as well as letting that person put a name to a face. If you will be mailing your resume, do so in a manila envelope. Don't fold it and stick it in a regular #10 envelope. You want it to look nice, so keep it flat when mailing.

- Try to keep your resume to one page if possible. However, if you have some important information that you think will put you in the running for the job and it spills over into two pages, that's fine, but you should NEVER have a resume longer than two pages!

- No personal information should be on your resume at all. Employers don't need to know your height, weight, and marital status.

- Be sure to proofread over and over and over again. And then do it one more time. Nothing makes you look more unprofessional than typographical errors on your resume. It makes you look sloppy and like you don't care. If you have typos on your resume, you won't get called for an interview.

- The resume is used to represent you and sell you to a potential employer before you meet face to face. It should represent you and reflect you in an extremely positive light. It should make you stand out among other applicants and urge the person in charge of hiring to want to call you first!

The Cover Letter

You will also need a cover letter to accompany your resume. In general, the cover letter should be as concise and to the point as possible. Don't ramble on and on, let your resume do the talking. The cover letter is just a basic introduction to your resume.

Use very positive language and be concise. If you are responding to an Ladies and Gentlemen:

I am writing in response to your ad that ran in yesterday's edition of The Tribune in which you advertised for a research assistant. As you can see from the attached resume, I have the qualifications you asked for in the ad and would like to be considered for this position.

While my previous career was not in the research field, I have always had an interest in working a job such as this which is why I have obtained additional schooling that qualifies me to do this type of work. Doing research has always been a dream of mine, and I was excited to see that your company has a position available.

I am the right person for this job which will be evident to you with a personal interview. You will see my passion and desire to work in this field when we can speak face to face. I can be reached or a message may be left at (555) 555 -5555. I look forward to meeting with you. Thank you in advance for your consideration!

Sincerely, 81

If you don't have a specific person you are addressing the letter to, you will want to address it to "Ladies and Gentlemen". DO NOT address it to "To Whom It May Concern". That is considered unprofessional and very non-businesslike.

Just as with the resume, you should proofread extensively to make sure that there are no typographical errors and that your punctuation and grammar is all correct.

The Interview

A good, solid resume and cover letter will get you an interview which is when it is your job to shine and stand out from other applicants. How do you do that? Preparation is key in the process. Being prepared for a job interview means knowing about the industry, the employer, and yourself. It means paying attention to details like personal appearance, punctuality, and demeanor.

What To Wear

First, you must dress appropriately. Generally, it's a good idea to wear a suit for a job interview. Go with something simple, in a neutral tone. The more conservative your field is, the more conservative your suit should be. For example, if you're applying for a job in an investment firm, go with a navy blue or dark gray suit. For women, a dress is also appropriate attire for a job interview.

It's a good idea to match your interview attire to the prospective job. If you are applying for a job working on a warehouse floor, you will look out of place wearing a formal suit. Keeping that in mind, dress a little better than you would for a day at work and make sure your clothes are neat and clean. Do not wear jeans.

Make sure that whatever you wear is clean and in good condition. That means no tears or stains. It should also not be outdated. A good, classic style and cut for a suit is a good choice since it's appropriate for many situations.

In all instances, wear closed-toe shoes. Sandals are never appropriate for a job interview, unless you are applying for a job as a lifeguard. Black shoes match everything (yes, even your navy blue suit). Stick with a conservative style. Women should not wear very high heels. Sneakers are not appropriate at all.

Women, don't wear an excessive amount of jewelry and take it easy on any makeup. You want to make an impression with you, your personality, and qualifications. You don't want to be remembered as the lady who piled on the blue eye shadow and ruby red lipstick.

You'll want to bring an extra copy of your resume along with your reference sheet. If you are applying for a job which might require you to provide sample of previous work, you need to bring that as well. You need to have something to carry it all in.

Leave the backpack at home. You want to look professional, not like you're taking a stroll across campus. A woman can carry a small to medium sized handbag. A man or woman can carry a briefcase if he or she wishes, or a folder or portfolio.

Questions

Once at the interview, you are going to be asked a lot of questions by your potential employer. They will ask about you in particular such as what your strengths and weaknesses are. You might want to prepare for answering questions by listing some of your attributes. Talk to former co-workers with whom you worked closely. Ask them to list some traits about you that they most admired -- work related, of course.

Try to find some faults as well. You won't, obviously, spontaneously tell a prospective employer about these faults, but you may be asked to. One question that sometimes comes up in an interview is "What is something that has been a problem for you at work?" By studying your faults, you will be able to choose one that is somewhat innocuous or could be turned around into a positive.

For example, I've always been a very organized person – almost to the point of obsessiveness. However, employers look at organizational skills as assets not liabilities. So in an interview, I would tell them one of my shortcomings was that I wanted to be too organized.

Practice how you will answer possible questions in an interview. You want to seem somewhat spontaneous, but you also want to appear self-confident. The way to do that is to rehearse, not exactly what you will say, but how you will say it.

A great method is to rehearse in front of a video camera. Study your posture, the way you make eye contact, and your body language. If you don't have a video camera, a mirror will do. Have a friend do mock interviews with you. The more you repeat a scenario, the more comfortable you will begin to feel with it.

When it comes down to it, isn't this the main point of the interview? Speak slowly and clearly. I tend to speak very quickly, so this is something I must pay careful attention to when I am on an interview. Pause before you answer a question. Your answers will seem less rehearsed and it will give you a chance to collect your thoughts. Keep in mind that a very brief pause may seem like an eternity to you. It's not.

Since the interviewer's job is to make sure that not only your skill, but your personality as well, is a good match, you must establish rapport with the person or persons interviewing you. That begins the instant you walk in the door. Let the interviewer set the tone.

Nothing is as awkward as offering your hand and having the gesture not returned by the other person. Therefore you should wait for the interviewer to offer his or her hand first, but be ready to offer your hand immediately. Some experts suggest talking at the same rate and tone as the interviewer. For example, if the interviewer is speaking softly, so should you.

It's alright for you to show your true personality, but be careful not to go too over-the-top. I am a very bubbly, naturally outgoing person who tends to get a little hyperactive in stressful situations. I also have a gift for humor which tends to make people feel comfortable with me.

In job interviews, I'll try to tone down the excessive energy that I usually have and inject some humor into the conversation. This helps relax both me and the person doing the interview and we're able to communicate much easier.

They say that body language gives more away about us than speech. Eye contact is very important but make sure it looks natural. A smiling, relaxed face is very inviting. Hands resting casually in your lap rather than arms folded across your chest also is more inviting. If you normally move your hands around a lot when you speak, tone it down some. You don't want to look too stiff, but you don't want to look like you're a bundle of nervous energy.

So what kind of questions can you expect during your job interview? Here are a few to think about along with some possible answers:

- Why should I hire you?

Because I sincerely believe that I'm the best person for the job. I realize that there are many other college students that have the ability to do this job. I also have that ability. But I also bring an additional quality that makes me the very best person for the job--my attitude for excellence. Not just giving lip service to excellence, but putting every part of myself into achieving it. In ... and ... I have consistently reached for becoming the very best I can become by doing the following...

- What is your long-range objective? Where do you want to be 10 or 15 years from now?

Although it's certainly difficult to predict things far into the future, I know what direction I want to develop toward. I would like to become the expert that others rely upon. And in doing so, I feel I will be fully prepared to take on any greater responsibilities that might be presented in the long term.

how it would actually apply.

- What is your greatest weakness?

I would say my greatest weakness has been my lack of proper planning in the past. I would over-commit myself with too many variant tasks, then not be able to fully accomplish each as I would like. However, since I've come to recognize that weakness, I've taken steps to correct it. For example, I now carry a planning calendar in my pocket so that I can plan all of my appointments and "to do" items. Here, let me show you how I have this week planned out...

- What attracted you to our ad over others?

I approach my job hunting strategy pretty much like I approach my work. I took some time to think about the skills I want to use on my next job, the industry I'd like to work for and the location I want. I did some research on companies that were advertising and knew this company had the qualities I am looking for in my career and future.

If you are interviewing for a sales job, it's entirely possible that the interviewer will ask you to sell him or her something. For example, I had one prospective boss who laid a pen on the table between us and told me to "sell" him the pen. What he wanted was to see how my persuasive skills were and if I could point out the great aspects of that pen to motivate him to "buy" it.

Usually toward the end of the interviewer, the person conducting it will ask you if you have any questions. You should have some. As in every other aspect of the job search, you are trying to show the employer how you can fill their needs. By asking certain questions, you are putting yourself in the job and showing the employer how you will satisfy the employer's needs. Here are some questions you may want to ask of the interviewer:

- Why is the position open?
- Are there any special projects I will be working on?
- How often will my performance be evaluated?
- Is pay tied to performance?
- What qualifications do you look for in a person who will be doing this job?
- What type of potential is there for upward mobility?

Don't ask about salary, benefits, or vacations, as those all imply "what will you, the employer, do for me?" However, the interviewer may bring up the question of money. He or she may ask what salary you hope to earn. You must prepare for this question before the interview. Find out what others in the same position are earning. Always give a range, not an exact number. This will help keep you from pricing yourself out of a job. You don't want the employer to think they can't afford you, but you also don't want them to think you are a cheap commodity.

There are some questions that the interviewer cannot ask you. That's right – they CANNOT ask you certain things and you are in no way obligated to answer them. Of course, if you want to tell them how old you are how many children you have, you can, but you don't have to do so if asked. Essentially, employers cannot ask questions related to any of the following:

- Race
- Color
- Sex
- Religion

- National origin
- Birthplace
- Age
- Disability
- Marital/family status

The reason they are considered illegal is because if they base their decision to hire you or not hire you on any of these factors, it is discriminatory which is against federal law. So how do you handle it when you are asked an illegal question? You have a couple of choices.

Answer the intent of the question instead of the question itself. For example, if you are asked whether you are a United State citizen (not legal to ask), reply that you are authorized to work in the U.S. which is a question the employer can ask you and which is appropriate to answer. Since you are not required to answer the question, it is well within your rights to refuse to answer it. If you refuse to answer the question, do so in a non-confrontational way that doesn't make you sound uncooperative.

You may want to say something like "With all due respect, I don't think that has anything to do with my qualifications for this job." If you refuse to answer the question, it could cost you the job, but would you really want to work for a company that would ask questions of you that are irrelevant and inappropriate?

After The Interview

After the interview, it is essential to follow up with a thank you note. This serves two purposes. First, it tells the employer that you are grateful for their time and want to do the polite thing by sending out a note thanking them for that. But, a thank you note also brings you back into their mind which can be good if they are close to making a decision on who to hire. It is also your chance to reiterate something you mentioned on the interview or bring up something you forgot to mention.

You should try to send a note to each person who took part in your interview. If you don't remember the name of each person, call the receptionist for some help. Keep your note brief. Make sure it is typed. Sending a formal thank you note sets you apart from everyone else who forgot to or chose not to do this, so it's a good idea to always send one.

And then, you wait. Sometimes you'll be asked to come in for a second interview with a different person before a decision is made. If you are chosen for the job, you will get a phone call during which time you can discuss salary and starting time or set an appointment to come in and do so. If you are not chosen for the job, you will most likely receive a letter in the mail that won't give you a specific reason why you weren't hired, it will probably just say something along the lines of "We've chosen someone else for the position". That's the worst part is not knowing what you could have done different to improve yourself the next time.

If you're comfortable enough, you may want to make a phone call to the person who interviewed you and ask just that – why weren't you chosen for the position? When you ask this question, don't ask in an arrogant or whiny way so that it sounds like you have "sour grapes". Simply explain to the interviewer that you are looking for ways to improve yourself and want his or her input.

You may also find yourself yearning to turn a beloved hobby into a business. Many people have done this and have realized great success.

Chapter 10

Turning a Hobby into a Career

(Return to Contents)

What do you like to do? Is knitting your passion? Do you love garage sales and can't imagine a Saturday morning without them? Maybe you have a real talent for cooking. Perhaps you love to use a computer and have found that it comes easily to you. If you have something that you love to do and seem to be good at it, it is truly possible for you to turn that hobby into a real career.

If you think it's possible that you want to turn your hobby into a career, you should start with a realistic business plan. Map out how you will start your business and where you want to end up so you will feel and be successful.

Yes, this writer has even turned a hobby into a business. I'm a multi-faceted individual! I've always had a love of garage sales and found myself with an excess of my garage sale stuff that I realized I would never actually use. That's when I found e-bay!

I started selling my stuff on e-bay and found that there was a real market for some things. It became an obsession. The more money I made, the more I became obsessed. I am now a Power Seller on e-bay and enjoy a nice side income as I substitute teach and write.

The thing about getting started with making a hobby into a career is to find a market and then capitalize on it. Have enough inventory on hand and then start selling what you create. E-bay is a wonderful place for people to start selling handmade wares and has provided a nice living for people who take the time to place their auctions up for sale.

You must have something that makes you stand out from your competition. That applies to businesses on e-bay or on your own. Think about providing an additional service or some extra that will make it worth the buyer's time to purchase your product. Many a successful business has been successful just because they go that one extra step that makes them stand out.

Networking can be very important when you are trying to grow your hobby as a business. Try bringing your wares to a local business and see if they will be willing to partner with you in sales. You give them a commission and they carry your product in their store. Not only does this give you a market share in your locality, but it helps spread the word about what you are making and selling.

Remember that if you are self-employed, you should be putting some of your profits away to pay self-employment taxes. The last thing you want is for the government to come after you for the taxes that you should be paying. While there are income guidelines as to what you are required to report to the IRS, you still want to be prepared.

The thing about making a favorite hobby into a business venture is to be sure that you will still enjoy it even when you are making hundreds of them a week. Be prepared for popularity and know that you will still love doing what you do after you are successful.

The best part about making your beloved hobby into a business venture is that you will be your own boss! You can work when you want, rest when you want, and enjoy the fruits of your efforts. Sometimes it might be overwhelming, so be sure that you have what it takes to withstand the pressure and continue even when you're not really sure you want to!

Don't discount the experiences of others. There are plenty of people who have made millions of dollars just by taking something they love to do and turning it into an empire (so to speak). Read up on them and take the advice that they have to give. It's always nice to have a mentor, so capitalize on their mistakes and successes and then learn from the mistakes while embracing the successes. Model your own home business on those who have found out the secret to making money without sacrificing your sanity!

You will also want to look into government grants that are available for small businesses. Check online for places that will entertain your request for funds to start your own home business. The government is very happy to offer up funds that will help everyday people start their own business and you deserve those funds just as much as anyone else!

Turning a hobby into a business can be a very amazing way to not only generate cash for yourself and your family, but it is also a way to allow you to work from home and do what you love doing. I'm not sure anyone would turn down free cash so that they could work a job that they love and on their own terms!

Conclusion

Making a career change is a scary step. At least it can be! But when you are unhappy with what you are doing, why shouldn't you go after your dreams and take a stab at something that you are pretty sure you will love while getting paid for it?

The key is to be confident about what you want to do and then just go for it! If you need to take some classes to work where you want to work, then do it. It doesn't matter how old you are – or how young you are. You can make a career change anytime and under any circumstances. It'll just take commitment and a little hard work, but it can be done.

www.ingramcontent.com/pod-product-compliance
Lightning Source LLC
Chambersburg PA
CBHW060435220526
45465CB00008B/3153